The Lizard Paradigm and Other Proverbs

ISBN
978-34233-7-1

INTRODUCTION

<u>What are Proverbs?</u>

Proverbs are short utterances full of meaning expressing commonly held ideas and beliefs. They are soundly rooted and reflect the oral traditions of people. Except for the Bushman of South Africa and Nilotic people, according to Finnegan (1970:389)[1], all cultural groups in Africa have proverbs. Sometimes it is difficult to distinguish between a proverb, a saying, a proverbial simile, an adage, an epigram and a wise saying, because they have similar functions, and more so because proverbs can be viewed from many angles that are not necessarily literary– philosophical for instance, or religious or historical etc.

<u>How Do Proverbs Evolve?</u>

How proverbs evolve is still debatable and not very clear, but they are generally regarded as developing from distilled experience of common men and reflections on issues and ideas by sages and opinion leaders and from oral traditions. This supposition can be accepted if one recalls how for instance during political periods when campaigns are intensive, words and powerful expressions are coined.

Janet Heseltine (1963)[2] in a discussion about how proverbs come into existence, suggests that they first come as the experiential reflections and utterances by opinion leaders such as the example cited above or a distillation of experience by a common man in a form of comment e.g.

> 275. He who is bothered shakes off the morning
> dew

---

[1] Finnegan, R. (1970) <u>Oral Literature in Africa</u>, OUP

Or observation of nature e.g.

67. The generosity of termites, giving out the wings
and escaping on legs

become familiar expressions as they are applied to similar incidences by those who heard from the first person or from the media as is currently possible. Subsequently such comments are further refined by oral performers or speakers like praise singers and opinion leaders. From then on, as they are repeated, they become proverbs and are disseminated anonymously by parents, teachers, wise men, and politicians.

Proverbs are Mobile

Just like there is language borrowing among cultural groups, proverbs are also borrowed through translation or the same kind of wisdom repeated in another language. In this collection the following proverbs appear to be borrowed from Hausa proverbs, there may be many others.

124 The fortune of a frog climbs not the tree
170 Exceeding the farm with seeds
294 He who Allah destined to be slapped, heeds not. "Be patient"

Proverbial Techniques

This collection also shows how Fulbe proverbs use intensive colorful pictorial form of expressions together with the general techniques of alliterations, rhymes, hyperboles and parallelism to illustrate a general principle using a particular situation. This penchant for using a particular situation to express a universal principle makes the proverbs striking and ingenious. Some of the notable proverbial motifs used to achieve poetic excellence in the proverbs are:

Direct similes e.g.

> 78. A woman is like a man, she lacks only the quiver
> 117. Beginning and end, like the tail of a frog!
> 131. Character is like rock carvings
> 251. An arrow in a body is like it is in a quiver

The most abundant technique however is allusion. Almost 80% of Fulbe proverbs are allusive.

> 8. The heart has no bone (human nature is weak)
> 13. A child can not carry a child
> 47. Intention leads to Mecca not provision
> 66. Generosity cannot cause poverty.
> 118. Beginning is not the end
> 244. The legs are resting, but the heart is not.

Another technique used is the metaphorical generalizations e.g.

> 9. The son of adversity knows only adversity
> 21. The sleep that finished the blind.
> 25. A shadow can't be buried
> 27. The talkative ends up paying the debt of his grandfather
> 77. Early riser escapes the sun etc.

One remarkable technique that must be mentioned is the use of quoted speech attributed to divine, human or animal characters;

> 42. "Allah creates some and damn some" says the warthog upon seeing the antelope
> 44. Allah says, "standup and I will help you"
> 65. The blind says, "Eyes smell"
> 109. "First and last!" says the vulture after a day's fasting.

249. The crane starts with the gall bladder and
     says, "Never again!"

The list of proverbial techniques cannot be exhausted in an introduction like this one, but they generally show how Fulbe apply imagination and insight to human affairs and the general interaction between the flora and fauna.

<u>Proverbs and Imagery</u>

That is why Arnott (1957:380) who studied a wide range of Fulbe folklore, notes how they are loaded with conjured pictures as against English and majority of other cultures that depend on 'puns and double meanings'. The proverbial expressions are made colourful and striking by illustrating a general principle in terms of a particular situation. The illustration is done by applying imagination and insight into situations and by playing of images and ideas in an odd way;

116	An entangle hyena licking potash (with the cattle)
67	The generosity of termites, giving out the wings and escaping on legs.
54	Mischievous mosquitoes harassing a sleeper
95	An amulet seeking frog meeting a ferocious snake.
165	The wind storm that met the frond already dangling.
179	An iguana rekindling hot charcoal.
192	A hunchback crawling into a tunnel.
213	A porcupine putting a saddle on its back and inviting a rider!
264	A morsel on excreta.

The striking images are endless!

<u>**Functions of proverbs**</u>

Having talked about imagery, one needs to finally comment on functions of proverbs. Proverbs are generally used as a rhetorical strategy to induce an appropriate frame of mind to receive a moral point, advice or to emphasize a point, etc. In that way the proverbs are effectively used for the transmission of Fulbe wisdom and social principles. The proverbs not only transmit wisdom and principles, they also embody Fulbe attitude to the flora and fauna of their environment. Take for example the common attitude of Fulbe to the hyena, In Fulbe folklore, the hyena is foolish, greedy, despicable and over confident. Ditto in Fulbe proverbs, 'uncle' hyena finds no respite!

> 114. A hyena also with cakes
> *(To show how someone is unworthy of something)*
> 115. A bare-foot hyena trotted on rough terrains, what of the one with shoes!
> 116. An entangled hyena licking potash
> *(When a creeping hyena is trapped in a cattle ranch, surrounded by dangerous bulls, what can it do but lick potash like other cattle to escape being noticed!)*
> 242. Whoever drinks hyena's porridge will die fleeing.

To be fair to the hyena one should also carry out such attitudinal analysis for other creatures like cranes, cats, dogs, etc given space and time, but generally, as a conclusion, proverbs whether among the Fulbe or indeed any other ethnic group conceal or emphasize ideas in speech. They ginger verbal interactions and help make a speaker distinguishable while elevating what could have been a mundane communication. Try to gauge, whenever privileged, how the insertion of a proverb amidst a conversation lit up people (a kind of joy in rediscovering a lost wisdom registering on their faces). One will have to add quickly however, that the use of trite proverbs (just like hackneyed sayings, e.g. God says, "standup and I will help you" etc) achieves exactly the opposite of spicing conversations, unless uttered in solemn occasions.

Aminu Hamajoda   *January 2016*

Proverbs

1. *Leaning against a granary assuage no hunger.*

2. *The past is never momentary! (often used when one exclaims "I just met him an hour ago!" upon the death of a close one)*

3. *The groom is striking, the bride groom is striking, the matrimony of scorpions.*

4. *Knowing the water pitcher is leaking yet fetching water with it.*

5. *They say here it is, you say here are its foot steps.*

6. *They say eat this butter, you ask is it grinded?*

7. *They lend you a hand, but you go for the elbow.*

8. *The heart has no bone (human nature is weak).*

9. *The son of adversity knows only adversity.*

10. *The son of a pauper tires not the itching of rags.*

11. *The baby rabbit fears not the plains.*

12. *The young carrier of flour is the friend of elderly travellers (cupboard love).*

13. *A child can not carry a child.*

14. *Like spanking on a boil.*

15. *Baobab tree begets irritating chaff, scholar begets a thief.*

16. *The dog says "Instead of idleness, better lick the testicles."*

Leaning against a granary assuage no hunger

17. *No matter how fast a hunting dog is, the monkey on a tree is beyond its reach.*

18. *The well is full, but the pitcher is broken.*

19.   *The donkey develops inflammation but it was the camel that was treated.*

20.   *Pulling aside is not always for counselling*

21.   *The sleep that finished the blind*

22.   *One eyed man is unthankful until he sees the blind*

23.   *Growing in rascality, the maturity of a baby donkey*

24.   *The shade of a palm tree is for the distant ones*

25.   *A shadow can not be burried*

26.   *This is only the fur wait till you see the owner of the fur*

27.   *The talkative ends up paying the debt of his grandfather*

28.   *The intensity of light cannot make the blind to see*

29.   *Getting soaked is better than seeking shelter from a ceaseless rain*

30.   *The tattoer who hates to be tattoed*

31.   *You can't hate the water pot but love the pitcher*

32.   *You can't see the elephant on your head but you see a louse on someone's head.*

33.   *As you weave forward it disentangles back ward.*

34. *Leaving excreta in the bowels, prevents no hunger.*

35. *The sign of doomsday starts at sunrise.*

36. *The sign of clouds that bear rain.*

37. *Sign of farm/onion is from the manure/leaves.*

38. *Good news to the cat the rat has developed hydrocele*

39. *When Ali did not limp, he went not to the mosque, what of when he limps.*

40. *With Allah everything is possible/ With Allah there is no difficulty.*

41. *Allah does not close and lock.*

42. *"Allah creates some and damn some", the warthog upon seeing the antelope.*

43. *Allah does not deform without reason*

44. *Allah says "stand up and I will help you"*

45. *Get the right partner, to get the right progeny*

46. *He who knows what you eat knows what satisfies you.*

47. *Intention leads to Mecca not provision*

48. *The pioneers were not fast, and the last were not slow- (death).*

49. One who starts ahead in eating will be ahead in satisfaction

50. The transplanted being better than the sown one.

51. A cock in hand does not crow

52. You cannot hate the pitcher and then love the water pot.

53. Like pant like trousers = Like cup like cover (Eng)

54. The mischief of mosquitoes, biting and ululating.

55. The only heir with a half share (of food)!

56. Before you taste the honey you must taste the bee stings.

57. By crawling does a baby start walking.

58. He can bake with water what if he gets oil!

59. The hungry man cannot giggle when the cook farts. = Hunger finds no fault with cookery (Eng)

60. Sweetness in honey, but value is in dates.

61. The joy that makes a thief to giggle in a granary.

62. Every bag has another that can swallow it.

63. The flies that make the excreter to flee.

64. The sack that tastes stronger than the salt it contains.

65.   *The blind says "eyes smell!"*

66.   *Generosity cannot cause poverty.*

67.   *The generosity of termites, giving out the wings and escaping on legs.*

68.   *The millet balls that escorted the curdled milk.(same kind can't help in emergency)*

69.   *Every big bird with its own dust*

70.   *I escaped narrowly is better than I was arrested with difficulty.*

71.   *The thief's mother cannot ululate twice.*

72.   *The eagle has gotten meat even before the death of the horse.*

73.   *The vulture has shaved even before blacksmiths fashioned blades.*

74.   *Circumstance that makes the goat to suckle a hyena's milk.*

75.   *Abortion is better than giving birth to a sluggard.*

76.   *Each crescent with its moon light.*

77.   *Early riser escapes the sun.*

78.   *A woman is like a man, she lacks only the quiver.*

79.   *Yesterday's lady has changed her wrapper = an old wine in a new bottle*

80.   *Next year's dairy cow should not die this year.*

81.   *Running and stopping is not a sign of bravery.*

82.   *Fleeing death and hiding in a grave.*

83.   *If a man gives you a goat don't deny him the skin.*

84.   *The giver of small will give the big (the small donor can be a bigger donor).*

85.   *Business had to be done even with enemies.*

86.   *The blood in the neck must rise to the head*

87.   *The rat never misses the way to its hole*

88.   *A heap of meat can't overwhelm a hyena's cub*

89.   *For a guy to be ashamed, better be a guest in heaven*

90.   *One with iron trousers squats not.*

91.   *An eagle in the air, a sand-fly in the air.*

92.   *Where a thorn pierces, that is where it is removed*

93.   *Better heard than seen.*

94.   *Crossing a river and dying of thirst*

95.   *A frog looking for a get-rich talisman; it meets a snake, and starts looking for a get-way charm.*

96.   *The assembly of birds is not the court of an owl.*

97.   *The assembly of cats is beyond a cockerel.*

98.   *The gourd in water, rising as you press down wards.*

99.   *A leper's cat tires not from being caressed.*

100.   *A cat knows where to dig and excrete.*

101.   *Fish does smell despite years in water.*

102.   *The lizard paradigm - four legs up but abdomen on ground.*

103.   *A hyena has howled, and a goat is missing.*

104.   *Even chopped one (wood) is not carried away talkless of the one being hewed.*

105.   *The axe has no regard for the owner's leg.*

106.   *A thunderbolt has struck a gun; a boom has ascended to heaven.*

107.   *Tripping over a pile of shit, no injury but full of annoyance.*

108.   *Marriage can be based on lies, but cannot be maintained on lies.*

109.   *"First and last! "Said the vulture after a day's fasting*

110.   *Strike and flee is not bravery*

111.   *If a sorrel is sourless after flowering, it won't be sour ever.*

112.   *To the owner of hydrocele it is not heavy.*

113.   *Just like a visitor's death- no decrease in population no increase in weeping.*

114.   *Even a hyena with cakes!*

115.   *A bare footed hyena has trotted on rough terrain, what of one with shoes*

116.   *An entangled hyena licking potash (with the cattle)*

117.   *Beginning and end like the tail of a frog*

118.   *Beginning is not the end.*

119.   *Turn a fight you can't handle into a play*

120.   *he who farts shall not be angry with the one who heard*

121.   *Acacia tree has sprouted in the harvester's house. (one who plugs)*

122.   *The caretaker of an elephant does not fear an elephant (i.e. familiarity breeds contempt)*

He who has not crossed the river,
laughs not at the one gnawed by crocodile.

123.   *When the enemy slays, friends hawk*

124.   *The fortune of a frog climbs not the tree*

125.   *The tortoise's fortune does not run*

126.   *The flea's fortune enters not water*

127.   *The mortal is boring, the dead is missed*

128.   *The cockerel that civilized the ostrich*

129.   *A hen never plays with a cat*

130.   *The cockerel that dug up a knife*

131.   *Character is like rock carvings*

132.   *The character of rice and the intelligence of beans (sheep in a wolf's skin i.e. hypocrisy)*

133.   *The Mahogany tree worm knows not the sweetness of dates*

134.   *The madness in the guinea fowl's head is also on the tip of a stick.*

135.   *Jovial eyes, black heart*

136.   *The eyes of a stranger no matter how large are not discerning.*

137.   *The eyes do not consume but know what fills the stomach*

138.   *Neighbourliness is contagious.*

139.   *Neighbourliness smells.*

140.   *Being together is not being in love.*

141.   *Truth is a thorny attire*

142.   *One-man-army or one-man-band*

143.   *A kitchen knife is not used to a scabbard.*

144. *A man is a thorny food, none eats, unless he is confident.*

145. *Hot but rotten*

146. *A gourd insulting a broken calabash*

147. *Deliberate act is worse than madness*

148. *Tie a pant equal to your waist =(cut your coat according to your size)Eng*

149. *Like taking side in a fight and becoming a target (take someone's fight and it turns on you)*

150. *A bone is chewed where it is softer.*

151. *Where there are woods, there are no fibers, where there are fibers, there are no woods.*

152. *Around an elephant's carcass, a dead rabbit cannot smell*

153. *Where the eye sparkles, is where cataract starts.*

154. *Bambara nut is a poor substitute for ground nut.*

155. *The requirement of a donkey exceeds not the incinerator.*

156. *The fulfilment of a satisfied man benefits not the hungry man.*

157. *Festive satisfaction can't last for a year*

158. *It is attention that sees, the eyes are only watery balls*

159.	*Big brother the Junior of the Wardhead = big, but worthless*

160.	*Gaining freedom yet seeking for power*

161.	*The unripe falling before the ripe one*

162.	*The wind that plaits, the water that scatters*

163.	*The wind storm that met the frond already dangling*

164.	*Dreaming of a feast fills not the hungry man*

165.	*Reject a gift, yet crawl to steal*

166.	*Security is no more, milk has killed a cow/ corn stalk has boiled a bushel*

167.	*Noise of palm fronds…..scares not*

168.	*A head in a thicket, may Allah save the eyes.*

169.	*The guinea fowl head is too small for three sticks*

170.	*Exceeding the farm with seeds.*

171.	*Like scratching the eyes with a leg*

172.	*However horrible a beetle is, prevents not a lizard to swallow it.*

173.	*The hay that ate the horse!*

174. *Fear the snake, beat a rope.*

175. *In the snakehead lies the danger*

176. *The mouth of a stranger is like a drum (strangers narrate experiences)*

177. *Salty mouth, potassium heart (pleasant words, bitter intentions)*

178. *The mouth that slays the throat.*

179. *The iguana that rekindles the hot charcoal.*

180. *The iguana is not a friend to water only the monitor lizard is*

181. *One which is liable to entangle knows how to untangle (i.e. Itself)*

182. *Yesterday's chill has gone with yesterday's firewood*

183. *A cripple goes not to war.*

184. *Only trotters trip over*

185. *Only in peace can you pray and supplicate*

186. *Silence means peace.= (no news is good news)*

187. *Even the owner of the horse prays for its death, what of the caretaker*

188. *The owner of the head keeps his tuft where he wants.*

189.   *The dare- devils die before the sick ones*

190.   *The owner of the flour is the cook*

191.   *The owner of the bed knows what bites him (at night)*

192.   *The hunchback crawls not into tunnel*

193.   *The battle vulture devour both the Muslim and the pagan corpses*

194.   *Like descending from a camel and riding a donkey.*

195.   *Idleness does not make a concubine pregnant.*

196.   *Dried wood knows the condition of a living branch but the fresh does not know the condition of the dry wood*

197.   *Fire is lit with dry wood*

198.   *The tall man waster of clothes*

199.   *A good Friday starts from a Wednesday*

200.   *Honey has turned into mashed leftover food*

201.   *A short limb cannot scratch the back*

202.   *A limb cannot be yanked off even if it decays.*

203.   *The length of a beard guarantees not going for a day without food!*

204.	*Hyena's mosque is out of bounds to dogs*

205.	*Cannot avoid stepping on long tails!*

206.	*Fulfilled man knows not how a hungry man feels*

207.	*The smelling one is scented*

208.	*Every fruit is to be plucked accordingly.*

209.	*Amazing! A camel in a bottle*

*The carrier of goods shouldn't
laugh at the one who trips over*

210.   *Neighbourliness in wood strives on fire*

211.   *The courting hen brought disaster to the incubating one (layer)*

212.   *It is already sour before it flowers, what of when it flowers….*

213.   *The porcupine's saddle is for dare devils*

214.   *The one destined to crow cannot be taken by the kite.*

215.   *Leaving what cannot fatten you, will not make you lean.*

216.   *Whatever stands will lie down finally*

217.   *What black hair did not keep, grey cannot take*

218.   *The hand cannot untangle the damage of utterances*

219.   *Even before the soap owner was born, an egret is already white*

220.   *What cannot be cut by a blade cannot be cut by a cornstalk slice*

221.   *Whatever enters the net is fish, even shellfish*

222.   *What is nourishing to a white creature is death to the black one.*

223.   *It smells what it contains*

224.   *Whatever devours a monkey can devour a dog*

225.   *The source of your shame is the source of your scorn.*

226.   *What devour goats can devour sheep*

227.   *When death hovers around, it is the pounder it seeks not the mortar*

228.   *Whatever you sweeten will be sweet.*

229.   *Whatever is hot shall cool down*

230.   *The guest who brings a bed is still a stranger who will depart*

231.   *Whatever is rustling in the grass, will eventually surface*

232.   *What the elders foresee, the youth even on treetop cannot see*

233.   *A wanton flood meets broken pieces of calabash (i.e. a walk over)*

234.   *An unprepared war, even thorns can turn it back.*

235.   *Whoever cooks the food of malice shall have remnants in his pockets*

236.   *Whoever discloses his affairs shall be exposed*

237.   *Even if it is old it is still a carved one.*

238.   *Even the monkey acknowledges the cocoyam farm*

239.   *Whoever does as he likes will not get what he likes*

240.   *Whoever climbs the horse of greed will descend in the house of shame*

241.   *Whoever decides to carry a leopard, make a cushion of cobra for his head*

242.   *Whoever drinks hyena's porridge, dies in fleeing (keeps on running)*

243.   *Blindman's legs tires not of tripping over*

244.   *The legs are resting, but the heart is not.*

245.   *Hyena's milk is for her puppy only.*

246.   *Legs trot not but on earth.*

247.   *Relationship is on legs.*

248.   *What is a blindman's palaver in the bargain of a mirror?*

249.   *The crane starts with the gallbladder, and says "never again!"*

250.   *"If you suspect just fly away" says the crane*

251.   *An arrow in a body is like it is in the quiver.*

252.   *The sense that returns only when the arrow is let loose (too late!)*

253.   *The flour of a miser finishes just in making gruel*

254.   *Work cannot be done without tools*

255.   *A borrowed tool cannot finish a project.*

256.   *The barber groans, the one being barbed groans too.*

257.   *Leanness exceeds not the bone.*

258.   *A safe path never seems too far.*

259.   *A stick bends, only when young.*

260.   *(Sign of) an edible fruit is from the flowers.*

261.   *A tick that dies of envying the fish*

262.   *A gazelle cannot jump, while its kid crawls*

263.   *Beneath a rock has no guarantee/security*

264.   *A morsel on an excreta!*

265.   *The deep-eyed should start weeping before his father dies.*

266.   *Only valleys are not in contact, hills do communicate.*

267.   *Hyena's market is not for a goat.*

268.   *The one given a left over, cannot reject a morsel.*

269.   *Buffalo's horn is only from the hunter.*

270.   *Die and be accused.*

271.   *Even a slave (male) has a bag of fried meat?*

272.   *Like a leaning corpse.*

273.   *You cannot omit salt and expect a delicious broth.*

274.   *Maturity of moonlight, escorts not (cannot take you home)*

275.   *He who is bothered, shakes off the morning dew.*

276.   *You have a ladle, still your hand burns.*

277.   *An elder surpasses a grinder, but can borrow flour.*

278.   *An elder vomits, but never pukes*

279.   *The immature that is bitter, the ripe that is sweet*

280.   *A donkey that follows the cattle to stampede/browse.*

281.   *When the donkey is dead, farting is over*

282.   *A goat never ties a goat.*

283.   *An old woman's purse never gets tired of tying and untying*

284.   *A hare is not an elephant's servant they only live in the same bush.*

285.   *A snake on the ground, a leg on the ground. (Enmity ensues!)*

286.   *For free is only for the sluggard.*

287.   *A sluggard is like a locust antenna, sharp but harmless/ cannot stab even butter*

288.   *Blunt (knife) shaves not*

289.   *I'm grinding, why do you consume the flour?*

290.   *I want to eat, but I don't want to be eaten.*

291.   *He who has nothing authentic, is left behind.*

292.   *He who surpasses not fetching, surpasses not stains.*

293.   *He who surpasses not robbing, surpasses not to be robbed.*

294.   *He who Allah destined to be slapped, heeds not "be patient"*

295.   *He who is given by Allah, surpasses who is given by father.*

296.   *He who is soaked by Allah, never dries.*

297.   *The one who escorts ensures not your arrival.*

298.   *He who Allah smeared with oil, will never be dry*

299.   *He who sleeps earlier than you, wakes up earlier than you.*

300. He whose mum cooks the broth, never eats his morsel dry.

301. He who never gives birth, is never reluctant to get up.

302. He who has not crossed the river, laughs not at the one gnawed by crocodile.

303. He who has not crossed the river laughs not, at the drowning one.

304. A hungry man cannot feed someone.

305.   He who does not give, does not get.

306.   The unlearned has graduated.

307.   He who has not kept anything, squats not.

308.   First timer in death died cringing

309.   He who never heeds warning, will hear "how is your body now?"

310.   He who has not eaten hide, cannot vomit fur

311.   If you have not dined with a person, you cannot tell his consumption of broth

312.   He who has not stored can not retrieve.

313.   He who has not matured, has grown old.

314.   Like the unskillful refusing to work (all for the best)

315.   He who is childless rejects not the bastard

316.   He who dislikes the crescent's position, can climb up and adjust.

317.   Who tells the muezzin it is already dawn?

318.   It got inflamed after being spewed on

319.   Who dares say the king's mother's head is full of lice!

320.   Impatience (envy) eats not a pagan's food.

321.   *He who has nothing can't get angry.*

322.   *Like hair plaiting on lice = what is done cannot be undone*

323.   *Slipped, but didn't fall is better than fell, but didn't slip*

324.   *It is size, the elephant surpasses the hare, but not living in the forest.*

325.   *He who tolerates the smoke, will reach the cinders.*

326.   *A patient man can cook a stone.*

327.   *The iguana's tolerance results in its skin being sold in the market.*

328.   *The patience that kills the donkey.*

329.   *Patience never fails.*

330.   *The pricked finger is the one to be licked.*

331.   *Not as she (hyena) loves the city, the city loves her.*

332.   *Neither the bag nor the locusts.(double loss)*

333.   *It is not marrying for the monkey (that is difficult), but lifting the loads up a tree.*

334.   *It is not always that a burglar's mother ululates.*

335.   *Not every cloud bears rain.*

336.   *Neither the hook, nor the fish. (Double loss)*

337.   *"Don't say he died, he was killed" (one and the same thing).*

338.   *It is not the fetching, but where to sit and eat.*

339.   *Already it was pale, (donkey) what of after being beaten by rain.*

340.   *Just interference, a kola-nut in a broth, doesn't make it delicious nor tasty.*

341.   *The cow says "better the blade than be a carcass"*

342.   *Those alike, fly together = (birds of the same feather flock together) Eng*

343.   *Traps frighten not a rabbit, only incarceration*

344.   *The left (hand) washes the right, the right washes the left.*

345.   *"I went in, but did not steal!" cannot exonerate a burglar.*

346.   *Have this is better than hang this on your shoulder*

347.   *What a world there is, but life is short.*

348.   *When has the concubine rested, talkless of dandling her child?*

349.   *The moon is not held but still visible*

350. *Better the lazy you know, than the new and fast you don't.*

351. *Better a rotten (bird) than an escaped one.(a bird in hand...)Eng*

352. *Better a small measure than none at all.*

353. *Better the unpalatable (food) than hunger.*

354. *Better to be called someone, than the son of someone.*

355. *Better look back and fart, than fart and look back.*

356. *Kettle-water does not get sour without a reason*

357. *Water does not wash shadow.*

358. *Water does not kill a fingerling.*

359. *Hot water is not a pond for tadpoles.*

360. *Begged water does not wash elephant's head/dirt.*

361. *The feathered one doesn't know a hole exist in a tree trunk*

362. *Courtesy in hardship.*

363. *It is tolerance that loads a camel.*

364. *The footprint of an elephant covers that of a camel.*

365.   *The wild plum is ripe, but the monkey's loin has broken.*

366.   *Blind man's plum should ripe in his pocket.*

367.   *Because the eagle flies, does not deter the sand-fly (midget fly) to fly*

368.   *Because the sorrel is sour, does not deter the hemp to be cooked.*

369.   *Staring eyeballs prevent not the gnawing of skull.*

370.   *Because the night is unpleasant, deters not the coming of dawn.*

371.   *Because hyena's pant is torn, the dog laughs not*

372.   *The malice of snake, biting what it does not eat.*

373.   *Like the beauty of sorrel on a refuse dump.*

374.   *The pit of lies is never deep.*

375.   *The curved hole suits the curved stick*

376.   *A cobra's burrow, whoever peeps suffers, least the one who pokes a finger.*

377.   *I'm bitten and I am caressed, are not the same*

378.   *A bell tolling for the unborn*

379.   *A farm of thorns is for metal shoes.*

380.   *The unbought (horse) that committed murder.*

381.   *Like fire on beards, everyone extinguishing his own.*

382.   *Fire in buttocks, has no extinguishers.*

383.   *Riches are akin to smoke.*

384.   *A patient's wealth finishes on the physician.*

385.   *Honey on a fingertip is better than a granary of excreta.*

386.   *However fast the gazelle is, it exceeds not the earth*

387.   *However pleasant dying on Friday is, waking up on Saturday morning is better*

388.   *However you hate the buttocks, you sit on it*

389.   *However you hate the elephant, you can not say it fills not a pot*

390.   *However sour sorrel is, it never becomes tamarind.*

391.   *No matter how greedy a person is he cannot swallow his tongue!*

392.   *However pleasant receiving is, giving is more pleasant.*

393.   *However bad a donkey's milk is, does not prevent its kid to suckle.*

394.   *However frightening a forest is, a squirrel never robs on the road.*

395.   *However much a cow has milk, you cannot milk butter (from it)*

396.   *However dark the night is, a hand never misses the mouth.*

397.   *However bright a lamp is, it is not brighter than the moon*

398.   *However big the corn ear is, it comes from the cornstalk.*

399.   *However beautiful the pants are, they are not better than the loins.*

400.   *However long a stump stays in water, it never becomes a fish.*

401.   *However far a town is, there is another after it.*

402.   *The ear heard, the heart declined.*

403.   *However long the ear is, it never exceeds the head*

404.   *No matter how time changes, an egret never follows a dog.*

405.   *A kid's ear scares not a hyena's pup.*

406.   *Ears taller than head, have you not seen a donkey?*

407.   *Hyena's ears, donkey never holds.*

The wild plum is ripe,
but the monkey's loin has broken.

408. *Ears cannot be borrowed, so that a squirrel may borrow the hare's*

409. *Bees have stung the talkative on the tongue.*

410. *If you eat and not fulfilled, then licking fulfils you not*

411. *He who eats the beans gets bloated stomach.*

412. *Eat according to your stomach size.*

413. *Eating from a filthy man is better than from a talkative man.*

414. *He who eats you, sees not your leanness*

415. *A (single) bean spoils the lot =(one bad apple spoils the whole basket) Eng*

416. *Yesterday's food satiates not today's hunger.*

417. *Self-assurance makes the elephant to swallow a pumpkin.*

418. *Removing pants without excreting, is a great shame.*

419. *He covered me with a basket (i.e. he cornered me)*

420. *The gourds have broken, the children did not drink*

421. *A lizard fears not the hollow of a tree.*

422. *Fleeing and scratching, tallies not.*

423.   *Hyena's buttocks are used to the dew*

424.   *The buttocks sit before the mat on the ground.*

425.   *Galloping horse from God, which (raises) no dust (help from God, has no obstacles)*

426.   *Courtesy makes the Fulbe to suffer(in silence)*

427.   *The pullo man, a bag of malice, he drinks water and bury the well*

428.   *A Pullo may lie, but never makes false proverbs.*

429.   *The end of a fish - starts in water but finishes in fire.*

430.   *A goat doesn't hate sleeping with its owner, but hates water on its head*

431.   *An egg between rocks = (a fish out of water)Eng.*

432.   *He who waits for a dish (of food) has nothing to do with a morsel.*

433.   *Wealth knows no obstacles.*

434.   *The carrier of goods shouldn't laugh at the one who trips over*

435.   *Carrying the tongue on head, does not make it bald.*

436.   *Tightness of pant prevents not diarrhoea.*

437.   *Tightness of a knot, prevent not a loss.*

438. *Hazard is never minor, butter can break a tooth.*

439. *You can hate, but never look down upon.*

440. *An excreta smells when you are bothered by it.*

441. *If you put two cobs in fire, eating one, then one will burn*

442. *Sambo, the first -timer at a war. = (Johnny just came) Eng.*

443. *It takes two to break a calabash. (it takes two people to fight)*

444. *Be disgraced, die and leave a bad name (shameful acts linger)*

445. *You parted with Inna, you did not reach aamada (double tragedies/loss)*

446. *An owl's happiness is roosting before sunrise.*

447. *A leopard wrapped in sheep skin.= (A wolf in sheep skin)Eng.*

448. *Water for soaking fibers cannot be dirty.*

449. *For lack of a mother, a baby suckles a grandmother.*

450. *Poverty prevents not rascality.*

451. *A bird killed by starvation, removes not hunger.*

452. *Father`s friend is never a son`s friend.*

453.   *The chaffed one (grain) is saved from being a seed (to be sowed)*

454.   *The sanctuary that is leaking!*

455.   *Hyena`s den is for her litters.*

456.   *A greedy man dies in shame.*

457.   *Don`t stand under a tree, and look up to chop a branch.*

458.   *A cock shall not attempt to crow like an ostrich*

459.   *Fear not material poverty for your brethren, fear the poverty of intellect*

460.   *Don`t rush to praise, you may not know how to condemn.*

461.   *Going round and round, like a fart in trousers.*

462.   *Poverty, hate it, they hate you for it.*

463.   *The rolling one never becomes numb.*

464.   *Expectation sustains the living one.*

465.   *Strike a tree to know where the monkeys are perching.*

466.   *Even he who squats to escape is in trouble, talkless of he who squats to swallow.*

467.   *Hewers of corn stalk, negotiate on their way.*

468.   One who escapes from hyena`s jaws cannot be shown the way home.

469.   A diligent man is a saved man.

470.   Scrutinize the water (level) and that of the flour balls

471.   Looking up at what cannot fall is exhausting the eye sight

472.   If the bride cannot ride a horse, let her not carry the luggage at least

473.   If they ask you to sniff, then it does not smell.

474.   If the heart desires, the limbs must serve it.

475.   If a blind man wants to leave early his escort has to agree.

476.   If a cow is not provoked, the broth will not be tasty.

477.   If you beat a man, don't deny him crying.

478.   If you are to fight a rainstorm, be armed with lighting

479.   If you fear what eats you, you cannot get what to eat.

480.   If you are pointed to a thing, but cannot see, shaking you cannot make you see.

481.   If you befriend a monkey, your stick entangles not on a tree.

482. *If you don't start when you dislike, you never reach when you like.*

483. *If you climb a tree, you must know how to climb it down.*

484. *If you are to dig a pit of malice, broaden it, don't deepen.*

485. *If God brings a killer, He will bring a saviour.*

486. *If you can swim in water, you cannot swim in mud.*

487. *If you walk, do not forget you crawled.*

488. *If familiarity is useful, water may not cook a fish.*

489. *Either the fisherman's excreta or the fish's excreta.*

490. *If the mouse steals, the locust bean cake also smells.*

491. *If someone surpasses you with pants, surpass him with gown.*

492. *If someone says the broth is tasteless, he must have gotten food.*

493. *Those who enter water, hide not their navels.*

494. *If the head is saved, nobody looks for the cap.*

495. *If the skull is fleshy, everybody should touch his own.*

496.   *If a thing is hot, it is about to cool down.*

497.   *If the mouth eats, the eyes are shy.*

498.   *If a vulture will get meat, one will know when an animal is skinned.*

499.   *If the loins are not equal, the waist beads will not be.*

500.   *Casualties are not counted until the war ends.*

501.   *If the village servant is not asked for meat, will be asked for spice*

502.   *If the forest is on fire, locusts don't bid each other goodbye.*

503.   *If the river denies you crossing, it cannot deny you going back.*

504.   *If a bastard is on a tree, get a pagan to bring him down.*

505.   *If a hand over stays in a hole, it found peace (inside).*

506.   *If a bee stings it is beneficial that of a wasp is provocative.*

507.   *If the elephants are away, the warthogs can play.*

508.   *An elephant in the forest breaking trees, prevents not a hare breaking sticks*

509.   *If the pullo man is good ask the monkey!*

510.   *The beggar who comes with a carrier!*

511.   *If parents do not discipline (a child,) the world will.*

As you weave forward it disentangles back-ward.

512.   *When hazard climbs up the shed, giving charity cannot bring it down.*

513.   *If salamatu rejects, jabamatu will accept.*

514.   *If death leaves (you), age will not.*

515.   *What millet balls do to yoghurt, is what yoghurt does to millet balls.*

516.   *Where is the meat, talkless of attracting flies?*

517.   *If what's easy becomes difficult, what's difficult will be easy.*

518.   *Your mischief is like one who carried her husband, leading her co-wife*

519.   *The worst has seen a new day! (Worse than before)*

520.   *So arrogant, like a donkey at a wedding*

521.   *Investigate the thief and investigate the chasers of the thief*

522.   *Climb (a tree) and touch, then climb down and prod the fruit*

523.   *Ride on a bull, and insult the cow*

524.   *Death is not to be blamed, an only child married with cornstalk bed*

525.   *Death of a dog surpasses sympathizing.*

526.   *Death changes not the locust's eyes.*

527.   *Spend the night where dusk meets you.*

528.   *Lie down for me to kill you, if you decline I accuse you.*

529.   *Carry me on your back, but don't touch my back.*

530.   *Missing someone does not change his/her character.*

531.   *A blow does nothing to a stagnant water*

532.   *The iguana has no friend, but the monitor-lizard.*

533.   *He who sleeps with hunger in a camp, does not oversleep*

534.   *Like assisting a lazy man in a fight, you end up crushing down with him.*

535.   *Your donkey has excreted a candy!*

536.   *A donkey amongst cattle.*

537.   *Carving a stone, one half breaks, and the other spoils.*

538.   *He came without being heard, and left without being seen.*

539.   *Hunger kills not a pullo; it is a pullo who kills hunger.*

540.   *In gourds' palace, there is no embedding.*

541.   *A goat's tail, drives not flies, and does not cover (the genitals).*

542.   A camel's tail is far from the ground.

543.   Too much repairs, spoils the monkey's baby

544.   Healthy talks, ill actions.

545.   Your talk is like water in a basket.

546.   A bed's beauty prevents not mat to be spread on it.

547.   Even incubating one is civilized, what of the hatched one.

548.   The white eyes of shame are better than the red eyes of fear.

549.   Throw away the bone, and get rid of the flies.

550.   Whoever burns his corn farm, knows the market for ash water

551.   Rinsing (the mouth) is better than having an empty mouth.

552.   Stepping on a paper is also increasing your height.

553.   Stepping on a frond plate is increasing your height.

554.   Hurry to spray it, before it sprays you. (Kill your enemy before he kills you).

555.   He who rejects a little, nothingness will fulfill him.

556.   You like, but pretends not to, yet your morsel is like a grinder.

557.   You like dealing with a fool, but don't want to beget
        a fool.

558.   Seeing is better than being told.

559.   Seeing is not as painful as being called and denied
        your share.

560.   Wanting to eat, can prevent fulfillment.

561.   Even if fire consumes a town chief, it is a sought
        after utility.

562.   An eye can see who it hates, but a leg will not go to
        where it hates.